Strong, Beautiful Girls

Beautiful Me
Finding Personal Strength & Self-Acceptance

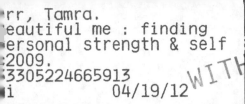

eautiful Girls

Beautiful Me

Finding Personal Strength & Self-Acceptance

by Tamra Orr

Content Consultant
Vicki F. Panaccione, PhD
Licensed Child Psychologist
Founder, Better Parenting Institute

Credits

Published by ABDO Publishing Company, 8000 West 78th Street, Edina, Minnesota 55439. Copyright © 2009 by Abdo Consulting Group, Inc. International copyrights reserved in all countries. No part of this book may be reproduced in any form without written permission from the publisher. The Essential Library™ is a trademark and logo of ABDO Publishing Company.

Printed in the United States.

Special thanks to Dr. Vicki Panaccione for her expertise and guidance in shaping this series.

Editor: Erika Wittekind
Copy Editor: Nadia Higgins
Interior Design and Production: Becky Daum
Cover Design: Becky Daum

Library of Congress Cataloging-in-Publication Data
Orr, Tamra.
  Beautiful me : finding personal strength & self acceptance / by Tamra Orr.
     p. cm. — (Essential health: strong, beautiful girls)
  Includes index.
  ISBN 978-1-60453-098-8
  1. Self-esteem in adolescence—Juvenile literature. I. Title.

  BF724.3.S36O77 2009
  155.5'33—dc22

                              2008011902

Contents

Throughout the series Strong, Beautiful Girls, you'll hear the reassuring, knowledgeable voice of Dr. Vicki Panaccione, a licensed psychologist with more than 25 years of experience working with teens, children, and families. Dr. Vicki offers her expert advice to girls who find themselves in the difficult situations described in each chapter.

Better known as the Parenting Professor™, Dr. Vicki is founder of the Better Parenting Institute™ and author of *Discover Your Child* and *What Your Kids Would Tell You . . . If Only You'd Ask!* You might have seen her name quoted in publications such as the *New York Times*, *Family Circle* and *Parents* magazine.

While her credentials run deep, perhaps what qualifies her most to advise girls on everything from body image to friendship to schoolwork is that she's been there, so she can relate. "I started out in junior high as the chubby new kid with glasses and freckles, who the popular kids loved to tease or even worse . . . ignore," says the doc. "They should see me now!"

Today, Dr. Vicki maintains a private practice in Melbourne, Florida, and writes articles for a variety of periodicals and Web sites. She has been interviewed or quoted in major publications including *Parenting* magazine, *Reader's Digest*, *First for Women*, and *Woman's World*, networks such as Fox, ABC, NBC, and CBS, and several popular Web sites. Dr. Vicki joined esteemed colleagues Tony Robbins, Dr. Wayne Dyer, and Bill Bartmann as coauthor of *The Power of Team*, the latest in the best-selling series Wake Up and Live the Life You Love. She is an adviser for the Web site parentalwisdom.com and also for MTV/Nickelodeon's parentsconnect.com. She is a clinical consultant for Red Line Editorial, Inc. Not to mention, she's the proud mother of Alex, her 21-year-old son who is pursuing his PhD to become a medical researcher.

With all that she has going for her now, it might be hard to imagine that Dr. Vicki was ever an awkward teen struggling to find her way. But consider this—she's living proof that no matter how bleak things might look now, they do get better. The following stories and Dr. Vicki's guidance will help you discover your own path to happiness and success, becoming the Strong, Beautiful Girl you are meant to be.

Take It from Me

If you had told me when I was in junior high school that I would one day write a book about self-esteem and personal strength, I would have shaken my head at how much you really didn't know me. I needed a book like that, so how could I possibly ever write one? I was a shy, quiet student in junior high, wanting little more than what you probably want right now—to be accepted. My elementary school years had taught me far more than I ever wanted to know about not fitting in, not standing up for myself, and not making friends. I was ready to put all of that behind me. I was just terrified I didn't have what it took to make the move.

It took me years to find the self-confidence to like who I was and accept that not fitting in with everyone else was okay. As an adult, I now realize it was more than okay—it was the best thing I could have done. Since then, I have become quite the rebel, focusing on doing what is right for me rather than what society tells me to do.

Having enough self-esteem to make your own decisions, walk your own path, and choose your own beliefs is one of the best qualities you can have. It is what makes you strong inside and out and determines what kind of adult you eventually will become.

Today, I am the mother of four kids, and I watch them and their friends struggle with some of the very same issues I did. They hesitate between wanting to be unique individuals and still trying to fit in enough to have friends and be accepted. What a balancing act that can be! Today, I am doing everything I can to help my kids walk that tightrope. I remind them that self-esteem comes from inside, and only inside. No one, not even I, can hand it to them—and no one can take it away, either.

I am delighted to be part of a book that tackles some of the issues that most threaten a young woman's inner strength and self-esteem. As mom to two young women myself, I have seen these challenges up close. Anything that is able to let girls know that they are not alone in their struggle is important to me. I hope you will recognize yourself somewhere in these pages. In doing so, I hope you realize that there are many choices in life to make—and each one helps you to grow up and become the strong, beautiful woman you want to be.

XOXO,
Tamra

1

Trying Out

One of the best parts of being in school is the number of opportunities you have to try new things. You find out about new jobs, skills, crafts, talents, and abilities and usually get the opportunity to try them out. It's exciting to suddenly find that you have a talent for something. The first time you sing in chorus or pick up the French horn... the first time you hold a baseball bat or swing a tennis racket . . . your first debate meet or outing with the ski club . . . each one of these moments is full of promise. You may be right on the edge of discovering something about yourself every time you try something new.

Unfortunately, sometimes trying out for something doesn't go as well as you had hoped. Despite your enthusiasm and eagerness, despite your high hopes and hours of practicing, you try out—and you don't make it. You don't perform as well as you had planned, others had more training and experience, too many people were trying out, someone else had more

When you find out that something you wanted to do is not actually your strength, it can be hard to handle.

passion than you did—so many possible reasons. But, no matter why it happens, not getting what you want can be depressing and discouraging.

When you find out that something you wanted to do is not actually your strength, it can be hard to handle. It's confusing—where do you go from here? Read on to find out how Nadine reacted when the results of her basketball tryout—and her height—weren't what she expected.

Nadine's Story

Nadine's older brother Nathan towered well over six feet (1.8 m). Schools had been after him to join their basketball teams since he was in third grade. Now that he was in high school, colleges had been sending him scholarship offers in hopes of getting him to enroll and play on their teams.

Nadine was tall, too, especially for a girl. Even though she was only 13, she was already taller than her

mom and almost as tall as her dad. Some of the kids at school called her the "giraffe." She could not buy clothes where her friends did because the pants and dresses were always too short.

She knew that her whole family expected her to play basketball like Nathan. It was just assumed. Nadine practiced free throws after school every day, trying to improve her skills. She begged Nathan to play one-on-one with her, but he rarely had the time.

Talk About It

- **How does Nadine seem to feel about her brother?**

- **Have you even been given a nickname? How did it make you feel when people used it?**

- **Has your family ever made plans for your future that you just accepted? Did you talk to your parents about it?**

In her lifetime, Nadine had witnessed countless games. Between seeing her brother play, attending the pro games that her father bought season tickets to each year, and watching games on television with her entire family, rarely did a day go by without Nadine seeing a basketball. That was perfectly fine with her, though— she loved every part of the game, from those amazing three-point shots to exciting overtime wins.

That's why what happened Thursday afternoon came as a shock. She had tried out for the school basketball team—and she hadn't made it. The coach had said she had all the height she needed, but not the speed. "It takes a player with both qualities to be on my team," Coach Connors explained. Nadine was crushed. How could she tell her family?

Talk About It

- **Have you ever been sure you'd be great at something, only to find out you were wrong? What did you do about it?**

- **How might Nadine's parents react?**

- **If you were in a similar situation, do you think your parents would be understanding?**

That night at dinner, Nadine's family had a surprise for her. "We know tryouts were today, so we decided to celebrate," her mom said. Grinning, she brought a cake out from the kitchen. "Ta-dah! Congratulations! Blow out the candles!"

Nadine did not know what to do or say. She just stared at the cake. She started to speak—and then burst into tears.

Nadine did not know what to do or say. She just stared at the cake. Then, she took a deep breath and slowly looked around the table. She started to speak—and then burst into tears.

Everyone's smiles quickly faded. Nadine's family looked concerned.

"What's wrong?" asked Mr. Hanover. "Are you all right?" In between her sobs, Nadine explained what the coach had told her that afternoon. Although she had expected her parents to be angry, they surprised her. Her mom and dad each put an arm around her and gave her a hug.

It was Nathan who really made her feel better, though. "Nadine, don't worry about your speed. I can help you with that, no problem," he said. "We can focus on that, and maybe you can try out again next time—or find another sport you like just as much."

Nadine smiled. She felt better already—or at least she did until she heard what her brother said next. "We can start at 5:30 tomorrow morning. See you at the track!"

Talk About It

- Why did Nadine think her parents would be angry? What helped her to feel better?

- Think of people in your life who might be able to help you accomplish one of your goals. What could they help you do?

- Which sports have you tried out for? Did you always make the team? If not, how did you react?

Working hard for a goal and then not reaching it can be really upsetting. You may feel very disappointed—plus you might feel as if you are letting others down at the same time. Keep in mind that you can get better if you just focus on the area that needs the most work. Find a way to make your weakness into a strength. You can always ask others for help, too. For example, Nadine's brother offered to help her improve her speed. She also could ask her coach, her PE teacher, or a friend on the track team to help her train.

No one can succeed at everything, but everyone can excel at something. Explore your options for how to improve at what you want. Set your ultimate goal as high as you want, and then set smaller objectives to achieve and celebrate along the way.

Get Healthy

1. Instead of keeping your feelings inside, share them with someone you trust. It could be one of your parents, your brother or sister, or a close friend. They might have a good idea for you.

2. Find an activity that you are really good at and truly enjoy. Look into different sports or other hobbies.

3. Keep trying out for the activities that you like the best. There will always be people who are better—and worse—than you.

4. If you try out for something and don't make it, set a goal to make it the next time. Think about what areas you could improve on before tryouts come around again.

5. If you aren't sure what your interests are, ask yourself what you like to do best when you have free time. That often holds clues to your talents.

The Last Word from Tamra

Trying out for something and not making it is never easy. But, giving up is almost never the right solution. Instead, you need to consider your options. Find something else to try, or find a way to improve so that you might make it the next time around. Having a goal to work toward will help you feel better about yourself. Everyone has some kind of skill or talent. Only by exploring the possibilities can you find out what yours is. Don't keep it hidden any longer!

2

Standing Up

Standing up for what you believe in is sometimes quite difficult—especially if you are going against the opinions of most of your friends or family. Maybe you think it is wrong to eat meat. Maybe you think cigarettes should be illegal. Perhaps you think people shouldn't drink. Or that kids should be allowed to pray in school. Whatever opinion you have, if most of the people around you do not agree, it can be very scary to stand up and say, "Hey, I disagree with you!"

So why do it? Why rock the boat and state your feelings about a topic when you know others will object? The fact is, those feelings are a big part of who you are.

If you pretend to go along with others even though you feel differently inside, you are lying to the world and betraying yourself.

Standing up for what you believe in takes guts. Keko felt strongly about something, but when she tried to get her friends to support her, she suddenly felt alone.

Keko's Story

Keko loved science. It had been her favorite subject for as long as she could remember. Her parents felt the same. Her mother was a chemistry professor at the local college, and Keko's father was in charge of the local high school's science lab.

For science class, Keko recently had written a report on how junk food could be really bad for young people. She did a lot of research online and at the library and was shocked to find out how many calories and how much sugar were in things she ate and drank often. She was more shocked to discover what these things could do to a person's weight and overall health over time. It worried her. She made a commitment to cut back on unhealthy foods and eat more fruits and vegetables.

Standing up for what you believe in takes guts.

At first, her friends agreed completely with her. They listened as she told them what was best to choose in the school cafeteria. They even agreed to give up dessert and replace it with fresh fruit. But then Keko went a step further.

Keko walked into the lunchroom with a clipboard in her hand. "I have a petition here that I would like you to sign," she told all her friends at the cafeteria table.

"Sure, Keko," said Tomas. "What is it?"

Quickly, Keko explained her petition. She was trying to get at least 200 signatures on it. Then she would send it to the principal of the school so he could present it to the school board. It was a petition to replace all the vending machines in the school. "The soda would be replaced with water and juice," Keko said. "The vending machines would only have healthy foods in them, like granola bars and dried fruit."

She paused—and was met with a thundering silence.

Talk About It

- **Why do you think no one is saying anything to Keko?**

- **What reaction do you think Keko was expecting from them?**

- **Have you ever felt strongly enough about something in your school that you wanted to work hard to change it? How did it turn out?**

Finally, the silence was broken.

"No chips?" asked Tomas.

"No candy?" asked Lindsey.

"Ummm . . . no," replied Keko, confused about the response she was getting.

"Then, no thanks," said Tomas, and the rest of the kids nodded in agreement.

"We'll keep our caffeine, sugar, and salt, thank you," added Craig with a grin.

Keko could not believe it. They didn't agree with her idea—in fact, they hated it!

"Wait a minute!" she said before her friends could get very far. "Lindsey, how many diets have you been on in the last six months? And Tomas, you just told me how the dentist found three new cavities! Don't you see? If we just change what we eat while we are at school, we can make a big difference in things like that."

Keko could not believe it. They didn't agree with her idea—in fact, they hated it!

Tomas, Lindsey, and Craig just shook their heads at her. They were not about to sign any petition like

that. "Seriously, Keko," Lindsey said as she got up from the table, "it's not that big of a deal."

Keko fought back tears as her friends filed out of the cafeteria.

"Excuse me, Keko," said Marcus. He was standing behind her and pretending not to notice her tears. "I'll sign your petition. I quit drinking soda for a month, and I was able to sleep better at night. I think your idea is good."

Keko stood up straight and took a deep breath. Having at least one friend's support made her feel better. "Thanks, Marcus," she said. "Now I have only 198 signatures to go."

Then Marcus asked her if he could offer a suggestion. "I was thinking that if the petition doesn't work out, maybe you could ask the school to offer some healthy snacks in the vending machines along with the junk," he said. "Then at least we'd have options."

Keko thought about it and realized it was a decent compromise. It would mean she and anyone else who wanted to could stick to healthful foods, and she wouldn't have to upset her friends. Now she just hoped the school board would go for it.

Talk About It

- How did Keko react when her friends left the cafeteria?

- Why did Keko mention Lindsey's diets and Tomas's cavities?

- What do you think of Keko and Marcus's compromise?

Ask Dr. Vicki

It is very important that you make good decisions and choices that are right for you, even if they are not the same choices that your friends make. It isn't easy being the one to have a different opinion or attitude about something. It takes courage to speak up and disagree with the people you care about and spend time with. If you feel strongly about something and truly want to make a difference, as Keko does, then finding the proper channels will help. You can start a petition, speak out at a parent/teacher meeting, talk to the school board, or write a letter to the editor. Sharing your ideas and thoughts on issues that matter to you makes you stronger and more confident.

Remember, it's also a good idea to respect the fact that other people have their own opinions. Just because your friends disagree with you on some subjects does not mean you can't be friends any longer. Keep in mind, too, that having your own opinions is fine, but forcing them on others isn't. You can't expect everyone to think your way—although sometimes it sure would make life easier!

Get Healthy

1. If you are going to stand up for what you believe in, be sure to have the facts to back up what you are saying. Some people will be convinced you are right if you have enough knowledge about the topic.

2. Remember that you have to do what you think is right, not what everyone else thinks. This takes strength and determination.

3. Find people who agree with your opinion and hang out with them for support and encouragement.

4. If you suspect your friends are not going to agree with your ideas, find a way to talk to them one by one and explain your concerns.

The Last Word from Tamra

Having the guts to stand up and say what you think takes inner strength and true commitment. Just keep in mind that other people's opinions matter also. Be willing to listen to theirs as they listen to yours. See if there is a way to come to a meeting of the minds—or at least a place where you can agree to disagree. Just because you may not see eye to eye doesn't mean you can't hang out together, as long as you are comfortable around them and continue to make decisions that are right for you.

3

Finding an Identity

Have you ever wondered if you might be a lesbian? Many girls do at one point or another. You might find yourself glancing at the breasts of other girls in the locker room or looking at other girls' bodies during sleepovers. Is this just normal curiosity, or is your brain trying to send you a message about who you are?

Being curious about other girls' bodies is nothing to be embarrassed about. Everyone is curious. You might be comparing how you look to how another girl looks. You might be wondering if your breasts are going to develop like your friend's did, or if you will ever have legs as long as the girl with the locker next to you. You might even be curious enough that you want to reach out and touch another girl—but that does not necessarily mean you are homosexual. Your interest could be just part of the growing-up process.

Maybe you've wondered about your sexual identity because you are not "boy crazy" like most of your friends. They are always whispering about

Maybe you've wondered about your sexual identity because you are not "boy crazy" like most of your friends.

some new boy and giggling if he even looks their way. You'd rather play one-on-one basketball with the boy than have him ask you out! Maybe your friends spend hours in the bathroom fixing their hair, makeup, and clothing, and to you, it just seems like a big waste of time. Does this mean something is wrong with you? Are you supposed to feel like them? If so, why don't you? Could you be gay?

Those are all good questions, and each person will answer them a little differently. After all, finding your identity is what the teenage years are all about. For the next five to ten years or more, you will be working on who you are and who you are going to become. Part of that exploration will certainly include finding your sexual identity, whatever it may be.

Liza sat down and talked to her mother about her feelings. She felt really uncomfortable doing it, but her head was so full of questions that she needed someone who could help her find some answers.

Liza's Story

Liza had a sleepover for her thirteenth birthday. She had a wonderful time. Her mom created a neighborhood scavenger hunt, and the girls had a blast running from house to house finding weird things like a safety pin, egg shells, and a quarter made in 1999.

Later in the evening, Liza put on a movie for everyone to watch. She'd chosen one of her favorites, about a girl who finds out she is amazingly fast and ends up winning the regional track competition. Liza loved watching how the girl trained each day. She noticed, however, that most of her friends paid a lot more attention to the girl's boyfriend than they did the girl. They kept talking about how cute he was— something Liza had never really thought about before. The other girls also chatted endlessly about how the girl's hair looked when she ran, what kind of makeup she wore, and the fact that she never got the chance to wear anything cool in the movie. Liza was shocked. She had never noticed the girl's hair or clothes before. Was there something wrong with her?

Talk About It

- **Why did Liza choose the movie she did for her party?**
- **Why is she surprised by her friends' reactions to the movie?**
- **Why does Liza wonder whether something is wrong with her?**

Later that night, after Liza's parents had told the girls good night, they all pulled out their blankets and pillows. Everyone changed into pajamas or nightgowns. As they did, Liza realized that some girls changed very carefully, making sure that no skin ever showed, while others just took off their clothes without much thought. She could not help but notice the incredible difference in the size and shapes of their breasts. No two girls were alike.

She found it fascinating but then suddenly felt unsure. Why was she looking at other girls' chests? Could she possibly be gay? The thought shocked her. It made sense, though. It explained why she wasn't as interested in boys as her friends. Liza felt like she was going to panic, so she went in the bathroom to take a few deep breaths and calm down.

Talk About It

- Why did Liza suddenly think she might be gay? Why did the idea scare her?

- Why do you think some of the girls were so careful when they were undressing, and others didn't seem to care?

- Have you ever looked at other girls' breasts? Why do you think you did it?

- Have you ever asked yourself if you might be gay? How do you feel about the idea?

"Liza, come back out here!" yelled Kathy. "We're getting ready to play Truth or Dare. We don't want to start without you."

Liza was not crazy about the game, but it was a tradition to play it at almost every sleepover she had ever been to.

"Hurry up, Liza," called Chloe. "I have one already. Lindsay—do you pick truth or dare?"

Lindsay grinned. "Truth," she said.

"Do you actually have a crush on your older brother's best friend? That's what Jennifer told me."

Liza was not crazy about Truth or Dare, but it was a tradition to play it at almost every sleepover she had ever been to.

Lindsay's face turned as red as her pajama top. "I . . . I . . . ," she stumbled. "Okay, yes, I do," she finally admitted. For the next ten minutes, all the girls asked Lindsay questions. What does he look like? How old is he? Have you ever talked to him?

Then it was someone else's turn.

"I'll go," said Liza. She paused. "Kathy, truth or dare?"

"Hmmm, I'll take truth this time," replied Kathy.

"Okay . . . have you ever wondered if you were a lesbian?"

"Why would you ever ask such a weird question?" asked Kathy, giggling.

Talk About It

- **Why do you think Liza didn't want to play the game?**
- **Why did Liza ask Kathy this question? What do you think Kathy will say?**
- **Have you ever played Truth or Dare? What did you like or not like about it?**
- **How do you think Kathy might feel about that question?**

"I just wondered," said Liza softly. Maybe asking that question had been a really stupid move.

"Of course not," replied Kathy. "That was an easy one."

The rest of the night went quickly. By the time Truth or Dare was over, the girls were getting sleepy. After sliding under their blankets and joking around for another thirty minutes, they all finally went to sleep.

A week later, Liza was still thinking about what had happened. She decided at last to talk to her mother about it. She hoped that her mom would not freak out and just answer her questions. Liza knew she would feel better about things if she shared them with someone who truly loved her.

Talk About It

- Why is Liza still thinking about what happened at her party? What advice would you have for her?

- What do you think Liza will ask her mother? Why did she decide to share her worries with her mom?

- Do you have someone you love and trust who you can go to with questions about your sexual identity? What questions would you ask?

- Have you ever noticed that your friends seem to pay more attention to boys than you do? How did you feel about that?

It is very common for girls your age to wonder about their sexual identity. In fact, it is normal for girls to want to look at or touch each other's bodies, or even want to kiss each other. It's all part of exploring and experimenting. Just because you aren't interested in boys, clothes, and makeup, or are curious about another girl's body, does not mean you are gay. But, feeling attraction for another girl may, in fact, indicate that you are gay.

Being gay is not bad or wrong. It is simply who you were born to be. Nothing makes you gay, and there's nothing you can do to stop being gay. It's not a choice; it's just part of who you are.

Talking to your parents can be a great way to get some of your questions answered. If you are worried about how they might react, you might try talking to an older sister or other relative about it, or even a friend's mom or guidance counselor. The important thing is that you do talk to someone so you can get the answers you need.

Get Healthy

1. Your sexual identity is as public or as private as you want. You can choose to tell a lot of people or just a few people close to you.

2. Remember that being gay may be a part of who you are, but it doesn't define you as a whole, no more than being straight defines the girls who like boys.

3. Keep in mind that curiosity about sex (straight or gay) and human bodies (male or female) is normal. Just wanting to see, touch, and understand any of it does not mean there is anything wrong with you.

4. Take the time to find someone you trust and ask questions. If you cannot find such a person, go to the library and find a book that can help you.

The Last Word from Tamra

Wondering if you could be a lesbian simply because you aren't into boys yet, or you prefer sports to makeup, or you occasionally look at another girl's body, is understandable. But you should realize that straight girls do the very same things. Whether or not you discover you are gay, it helps to know that being gay does not mean there's something wrong with you. Being straight or gay isn't a choice; it's just who you were born to be.

4

Owning Up to Mistakes

As you get older, you will be expected to act more maturely and take on more responsibilities. At first it may be just chores at home or increased homework. Perhaps it is remembering to put your books in your backpack in the morning or keeping track of your lunch money. As you get older, that list might grow to include a part-time job, babysitting, and other duties. Responsibility is a part of life for many years—so you might as well get used to it.

Have you ever had to own up to actions you wish you hadn't taken? It isn't easy. Maybe you'd rather blame fate, your brother, or even the dog. But the more mature thing—the responsible thing—is to admit you made a mistake and then do whatever you can to repair it. That is a lesson Teresa was not ready to learn yet, and the consequences were worse than she had imagined.

Teresa's Story

Teresa had just moved to the area and was still trying to get used to her new school. She had met a few kids, and they had been fairly friendly, but they were also into things that Teresa wasn't. They all smoked weed—some of them every day. Teresa had never even come close to weed. The wildest thing she had ever done was steal a taste of her mother's wine at a

Teresa had never even come close to weed. The wildest thing she had ever done was steal a taste of her mother's wine at a family New Year's Eve party.

family New Year's Eve party. Teresa's innocent behavior was all about to come to an end. The new kids told her that if she wanted to hang with them, she had to supply the cash for the weed this time. Teresa didn't want to agree, but she didn't want to sit alone at lunch again, either. She also didn't want to walk home alone at the end of the school day again. So she agreed.

Talk About It

- **What was the main reason Teresa agreed to get the money to pay for the pot?**

- **Have you ever agreed to do something just so you would fit in and have friends? What were the consequences of those actions?**

- **What do you think will happen next?**

Quietly, Teresa snuck into her mother's bedroom while her mom was busy making dinner. She opened her purse and took out two $20 bills. "That should be enough," she thought. Teresa stuffed the money into the front of her backpack and then headed for the front door.

"I'm gonna go meet some friends!" she yelled behind her. "Back by dinner."

Fifteen minutes later, Teresa was handing the money over to Theo, and he turned around and handed it to someone Teresa didn't recognize. The man handed Theo a baggie and quickly walked away. Soon Theo, Janet, Mallory, and Julio were busy rolling up the weed inside small white papers and lighting them. When they passed a joint to Teresa, she was not sure what to do with it. It felt strange in her hand. She wanted to drop it on the ground, but everyone was watching her, so she lifted it to her lips and sucked in. As she started coughing, someone suddenly yelled, "Cops! Get out of here!"

Talk About It

- Have you ever stolen money from someone? How did you feel about it?

- Have you ever found yourself in a position where you were scared and didn't know how to get out of it? What did you do?

- Have you ever done something illegal and worried about being caught? What happened?

Teresa froze, forgetting that the joint was still in her hand. All the other kids had disappeared into the nearby woods, and she was standing alone in the rotating blue and white lights of a police car. Her hands were handcuffed behind her, and she was shoved into the backseat of the police car. When the officers asked where she lived, Teresa could hardly stop crying long enough to give them her address. She could not imagine what her mother and father were going to say when they found out she had been charged with possession of drugs.

What could she do to escape this? How could she show her parents that this was not her fault? This was nothing but an accident, and she was innocent—wasn't she? This was the worst mess she could possibly imagine, but there must be a way to get out of it. She would be happy to name names to the police. One way or another, Teresa would find a way to get out of this.

Unfortunately, the police weren't too sympathetic. The officer who booked her didn't seem to be interested in hearing about whose idea the weed was. She found out the penalty for a first offense might involve a fine and community service.

Talk About It

- **Why does Teresa think she is innocent? What does she plan to do to escape blame?**

- **Have you ever tried to blame a big mistake on someone else? What happened when you did?**

- **What happens if you don't take responsibility for your actions?**

When her parents arrived to pick her up from the police station, her mother was in tears, and her father barely looked at her. On the way home, she tried to explain to them that it was the other kids' fault for pressuring her to try it and then running away when the police showed up.

"I didn't even want to do it," Teresa told them. "And it was disgusting!"

Finally her father spoke. "Oh, well as long as you didn't enjoy it," he said sarcastically.

"I don't care whose idea it was," her mother said. "You lied to me, you stole from me, and you disappointed me. And the fact that you're not accepting any responsibility for your own actions shows me you're not the girl I thought you were."

The next day, when everyone had calmed down, Teresa's parents told her what they had decided her punishment would be. She was grounded, of course. If there was a fine, she would have to pay her parents back by giving up her allowance and doing extra chores. And to earn back the privileges she had had before, she would have to prove to her parents they could trust her again. It turned out getting out of this wasn't going to be as easy as Teresa thought, after all.

Talk About It

- Did Teresa's parents' reaction surprise you? Why? Do you think the consequences fit the offense?

- If Teresa hadn't tried to escape blame, how could the outcome have been different?

- How do you think your parents would have reacted in this situation?

t's common to make a decision that you normally would not have made when you are trying hard to fit in. You might think the advantages—in this case, having friends—outweigh the risks. But in the long run, your choices catch up with you—either you get caught, or you are left with feelings of guilt. Before you make a choice that doesn't feel right, ask yourself: If this is what it takes to be someone's friend, then do I really want that person as a friend?

Making a poor decision is not the end of the world, but lying about it makes matters worse. Even if other people were partially at fault, it's important that you recognize your own share of the blame. It takes a mature confident person to be willing to admit when she is wrong and to take the steps to correct the situation. You will make mistakes ... everyone does. Taking responsibility for them helps you grow. Believe it or not, you can even make yourself and others proud—not of what you did but of how you handled it.

Get Healthy

1. If you are new to an area and feeling lonely, let your parents know. Talk to your counselor at school. There are ways to get connected with others that won't put you at risk.

2. If something feels wrong in your gut, chances are it is. Listen to your instincts and don't do it. If you're tempted, find someone you trust to talk to about it.

3. If you find yourself in trouble, lying about it to escape blame will only get you into bigger trouble. 'Fess up and take the consequences. It will probably be a hard lesson, but it also will be one you'll never forget.

The Last Word from Tamra

Everyone makes mistakes. That's part of human nature. If we're paying attention, we learn our lesson and come out a better person for the experience. If we try to escape our mistakes, and blame others, we don't learn. Instead we just keep running to escape them, and in the process, we don't really grow up.

When you make a mistake, admit it and then start dealing with it. It's the mature thing to do, and part of your job as a young person is to keep maturing. Taking responsibility for your actions is also part of what leads to healthy self-esteem and inner strength.

5

Trying to Fit In

Being a teenager is hard. Being a teen with some kind of physical challenge can be even harder. At this age, kids typically spend a lot of time and effort trying to fit in with the crowd. If you have any kind of disability, blending in can seem almost impossible. Your disability may cause you to move differently, learn differently, or communicate with others differently. Coping with the condition takes skill, adjustment, and time. It may mean you have to wear extra equipment, take certain medications, or make special arrangements to get from place to place. All this sets you apart from others—which in turn can make you feel like an outsider.

Even after you've gotten completely comfortable with your challenge, you probably are aware that it might make other people uncomfortable. They might not know how to talk to you or how they should act around you.

Romiko knows just what this is like. She has had to deal with a disability since she was very small. It has made her stick out in ways that she doesn't like, but she hasn't known what to do about it, either.

Romiko's Story

When Romiko was very young, she fell and hit her head on some cement steps. She was rushed to the hospital, and the doctor said she had a skull fracture. The accident not only hurt Romiko's head but also caused her to lose most of her hearing. This loss of hearing affected her ability to learn to talk. Because she couldn't hear other people speak, she never learned to copy the sounds they made. So when she tried to speak, her words weren't as clear or understandable as everyone else's.

The accident not only hurt Romiko's head but also caused her to lose most of her hearing.

When she was three years old, she was given her first hearing aids, and she had been wearing them ever since. She was used to them, but she knew they looked strange attached to her ears, and that made her self-conscious.

Romiko could speak quite a few words, but she knew her voice did not sound like other people's. She could use sign language very well, but almost no one outside her family could. Although she learned to read people's lips to understand what they were saying, Romiko felt uncomfortable trying to talk to other students—especially boys.

Talk About It

- Why does Romiko feel so uncomfortable talking to other people? Why might other people feel uncomfortable talking to her?

- Do you have any kind of disability? How do you feel about it? Does it make it harder for you to fit in?

- Do you know anyone with a disability? How do you treat that person?

In Romiko's science class, all the students were divided into pairs to work in the science lab. Romiko had been paired with Cameron, the boy she had had a wicked crush on for weeks. They were supposed to work together on this new experiment, but every time Cameron tried to talk to her about the directions, Romiko got confused. She couldn't read his lips very well because he didn't look at her, and the lab book was on his side of the table, so she couldn't read what it said. She knew all she had to do was explain to Cameron that if he'd move the book, she could follow along better. She also knew she'd be able to understand him if he looked right at her, but she wasn't sure if that was a good idea.

Every time Cameron tried to talk to her about the directions, Romiko got confused.

The following Monday, the bell rang, and lab started. Romiko hopped up on her usual stool next to

Cameron. Right away she noticed that the lab book was in the middle of the table. The second thing she noticed was that Cameron was looking straight into her eyes. She could feel the blush start at the top of her head and go all the way down to her toes. What was he doing?

Talk About It

- **Why is Romiko so uncomfortable with Cameron?**
- **Have you ever had to work closely with someone you had a crush on? How did you handle it?**
- **What advice would you give Romiko?**

"Hi, Romiko," he said to her. He made a point of speaking slowly. "How are you today?" As he spoke, he signed—Romiko could not believe her eyes. "My mom works with someone who's deaf," Cameron explained. "Over the weekend, she took me to meet him, and he taught me some basics."

Romiko giggled at how he was trying to match his signing with his words. "Yeah, I am pretty slow at it," admitted Cameron.

"No," said Romiko as clearly as she could. "You are just right!"

Talk About It

- What did Romiko mean when she told him, "You are just right"?

- Have you ever taken the time to learn how to communicate with someone who has a physical challenge? What was his or her response?

- Have you ever been in a position where others have had to find an alternative way to communicate with you? How did it feel?

We all have aspects of ourselves that we don't like or that embarrass us. For most of us, our flaws don't get in the way of how we function from day to day. But having an actual disability often means making some big adjustments just to get through everyday life. It may mean using a walker or a wheelchair, getting special help in reading, or wearing thick glasses. Romiko's disability meant she talked differently and needed to wear hearing aids. Being different at this age may make you feel ashamed and inferior. But a disability doesn't make you less of a person. It just makes you different in a particular way.

Romiko isn't defined by her disability. She's a regular junior high student who happens to have a hearing problem. If you see yourself as limited by your disability, then other people will see you that way, too. Other kids will take their cues from you. Learning to accept yourself, disability and all, will allow you to be confident. What Romiko needs to learn is how to let others know how they can help, without feeling embarrassed. For example, saying, "Excuse me, but it helps me understand you if I can read your lips," would let others know what she needs in a matter-of-fact, confident way. When you accept who you are, others will, too. And you will find that when you tell others what you need, they are usually very willing to help out.

Get Healthy

1. Focus on what a special person you are rather than on how different you are. Believe in yourself, and others will follow.

2. Everyone is different in some way—perhaps your differences are just a little more obvious than others. Show people how great you are regardless of your disability. This helps build your confidence, and people will notice.

3. When you talk to people, maintain eye contact. This makes a stronger connection, and they will be able to relate to you better.

4. When you act uncomfortable, shy, embarrassed, or awkward, others tend to feel the same way. Let the real you shine through!

The Last Word from Tamra

No one can tell you that having a disability is easy—only you know what it is like to live with and deal with one on a daily basis. Just remember that if you project confidence and a positive attitude about your disability and who you are as a person, others will follow. Give people a chance. Often they are not trying to be unkind, but they are just not sure how to respond to you. Be patient with them and appreciate the efforts they make. Don't let a disability hold you back from the world or from the people you want to know.

6

Getting Down on Yourself

Sometimes it may feel like life is nothing but pressure, pressure, and more pressure. You feel you have to meet your parents' expectations— as well as those of your teachers and your friends. Hey, even your dog expects you to take him for a walk, feed him, and play with him each day. When you add it all up, it can just feel like too much sometimes. You struggle to keep up and meet your responsibilities, but it isn't easy.

Can anything make it worse? How about having a brother or sister who seems to be good at everything? Or who gets straight As without trying? You know, the one who wins first place at the science fair, scores the winning soccer goal, or gets a full scholarship to college. Having an older sibling like that may make matters worse for you, since it seems impossible to compete or even keep up. And if you can't keep up,

The better your sister or brother does, the worse you feel and the more you may worry that you just aren't good enough.

what does that say about you? The better your sister or brother does, the worse you feel and the more you may worry that you just aren't good enough.

That's what Hannah was experiencing. Her older sister was everything Hannah wanted to be, and nothing Hannah did seemed to measure up.

Hannah's Story

Hannah looked at her older sister Victoria's report card. All As, as usual. Hannah couldn't remember a time when Victoria hadn't gotten straight As. Victoria was way beyond smart. She had gotten the highest score on her SATs of anyone in her school. She was graduating early because she had skipped sixth grade. If anyone in the family had a question, they asked Victoria. They knew she would know.

Glancing at her own report card made Hannah's stomach hurt. It wasn't terrible—but it sure didn't look like Victoria's, and it never had. Hannah was great in some subjects, and those As were easy, but she struggled in other classes, such as math and science. She usually got a combination of Bs and Cs. Why couldn't she be as smart as Victoria? Both sisters studied the same amount. They both did their homework. It didn't seem fair.

Talk About It

- **Why does Hannah compare herself to Victoria? How does Hannah feel when she compares herself to her sister?**

- **Have you ever compared yourself to one of your siblings? How did it make you feel?**

- **How do you feel when looking at your report card? Do you compare yourself to others?**

Hannah liked school, but she had to admit that her favorite class of all was chorus. She loved singing. She sang at school, at home, and of course, in the shower! Just this afternoon, the chorus director had asked her if she would be interested in singing a solo in the upcoming spring concert. Hannah was thrilled! She was so excited she thought she might burst. She planned to announce it at dinner that night, but before she could, her parents asked to see the girls' report cards. Of course, they praised Victoria for

another job well done. But her father frowned while mulling over Hannah's grades.

"Well, it looks like you're doing all right in most of your classes, Hannah," he said. "But what's with this C in science? I think you can do better than that."

"Maybe your sister could help you," her mother chimed in. "Victoria's always seemed to have a knack for science."

Of course, they praised Victoria for another job well done. But her father frowned while mulling over Hannah's grades.

That had blown the whole thing. Now Hannah just wanted to go curl up on her bed. She excused herself from the table and went to her room.

Talk About It

- Why didn't Hannah deliver her good news at the dinner table?

- Have you ever wanted to share something exciting with your family, but someone else's news overshadowed it? How did it turn out for you?

- What do you do when you're upset about something? Does it help?

There was a knock on Hannah's door, and she assumed it was one of her parents coming to see if she was all right. To her surprise, it was Victoria.

"What's up?" her sister asked. "You look pretty down."

Hannah was surprised her sister had noticed. When she explained what had happened at the dinner table, Victoria's eyes got wide.

"You're going to sing a solo?" she asked. "You are really brave! I would never, ever, ever be able to do that. I'd be scared to death."

Hannah was speechless. She could do something her sister couldn't? This had to be a first.

"Come on, let's go tell Mom and Dad," added Victoria. "They will be so excited for you!"

Hannah smiled. It sure was nice being the one in the spotlight for a change.

Talk About It

- Why is Hannah so surprised at Victoria's reaction to her news?

- Has a sibling ever been there for you when you needed it? What did they do? What was that like for you?

- What are you good at doing? Is there something you like to do that is different from what your siblings do?

Comparing yourself to others can be useful or harmful, depending on how you use the information. Measuring yourself against another runner on your track team to set a new goal for yourself is probably a helpful use of comparisons. If you compare yourself to the model on the cover of a magazine and try to make your body look like hers, that's not healthy.

The biggest mistake you can make is to compare yourself to your sister or brother and use that information to get down on yourself. Many girls think that if they are not performing as well as their siblings, they must be letting down their parents. But that's not true. Your parents would only be disappointed if you stopped being the best person you can be.

If you want to take a look at how you are doing and improve in some areas, go for it! But comparing yourself to someone else has no real value. Hannah will never be Victoria. Why? Because she's Hannah. The same goes for you—you are one of a kind. So, find your own special talents, gifts, and interests. Go after them and forget how everyone else is doing, because only you can be you.

Get Healthy

1. Remember that everyone has his or her own special talent—everyone! Find yours and get into the spotlight.

2. If you have a sibling who is exceptionally strong in some area, take time to figure out where he or she might struggle. It helps to know that no one is perfect.

3. If you are feeling overly pressured to meet expectations, talk to your parents or teachers about what you could change.

4. Figure out what you like to do and what you're good at—and go for it.

5. Remember that you don't have to be great at something to do it. Not everyone can be the star, but that doesn't mean you can't have fun!

The Last Word from Tamra

Comparing yourself to others is natural, and comparing yourself to your brothers or sisters is even more so. Just make sure that when you make these judgments, you are being honest. No one can be good at everything, but each person has a strength. The key to success is finding yours and making the most of it. If you act with confidence and enjoy yourself, you can bet others will be comparing themselves to you!

7

Feeling Awkward

Now is the time when you really start thinking for yourself. In the coming years you'll explore all kinds of decisions about who you are and what you do and do not believe in. You may also begin questioning beliefs you have grown up with. This can be particularly true about your cultural or religious beliefs. If you have grown up practicing certain customs or religious practices, you may be used to just accepting that things are done a certain way.

But what happens if you find yourself among kids who hold different beliefs from you? You may struggle between being true to your own opinions and trying to fit in with your classmates.

Just ask Lila. She and her family moved to the United States a few years ago from India. They are Hindus. Hindus believe in individual gods and goddesses known as Shiva, Vishnu, and Devi. While Lila likes being a Hindu, it was not easy when everyone else in her private school belonged to the Christian faith, which has very different beliefs and customs.

Lila's Story

Lila loved the United States. When her parents first told her that they were moving from India, she was worried about what it would be like. Now that she was here, it was wonderful. She liked the teachers at the private school, and she was doing well in her classes.

Lila's only problem—and it was a big one—was that she was having trouble making new friends. Back in India, she had no problem going up to new people and getting to know them. But there was no one else like her at her new school. Her parents had enrolled her at a private school because of the quality of the education offered there, but the school had no other students with a different color skin or a religion other than Christianity.

What happens if you find yourself among kids who hold different beliefs from you?

Although the other students were not unkind to her, they didn't seem to know what to make of her. If they weren't staring at her and making her feel uncomfortable, they were ignoring her. This had been happening ever since lunch on the first day of school, and she didn't know what to do to make things better.

The table Lila had sat at was occupied by a group of kids who obviously had known each other for a long time. A few of them said hi to her and asked her where she was from before turning back to each other. After listening to them talk, Lila figured out that they all attended the same church. That became even more obvious when they bowed their heads together before eating and said the same prayer.

Unlike the other students, Lila did not bow her head to pray. Instead, she closed her eyes and quietly said her family's traditional prayer: "Lead us from untruth to truth. Lead us from darkness to light. Lead us from death to immortality. Aum, let there be peace. Peace. Peace."

Talk About It

- Why does Lila feel awkward in this situation? What would you have done in her place?

- Have you ever felt out of place or different from everyone else? How did you handle it?

- Do you know people who have a different faith or cultural background? Do they fit in?

When she looked up, the rest of the table had fallen quiet, and everyone seemed to be staring at her. A few of the kids gave her weird looks. For the rest of the meal, no one said anything to her.

From that lunch on, Lila didn't feel comfortable sitting with those kids. Instead, she sat alone in the cafeteria or went outside and ate food her mother had packed for her. It was lonely, but she didn't know what else to do. She didn't like people staring at her.

As she ate her lunch, Lila watched the other students hanging out in groups, enjoying the time out of class. Every now and then, she caught someone looking at her, and she looked away quickly. She knew that kids were talking about her dark

For the first time since she had arrived in the United States, Lila felt homesick.

skin, her Indian accent, and her weird religion. Maybe America was not so great after all. Maybe she should talk to her parents about returning to India. She could live with her cousins. Lila felt a tear trickle down her cheek. For the first time since she had arrived in the United States, she felt homesick.

Talk About It

- Why do you think the other kids don't try to get to know Lila?

- What do you think Lila could do to encourage others to get to know her?

- Have you ever felt homesick? What did you do to make yourself feel better about it?

Lila was put in a difficult situation when her parents enrolled her in a school where the majority of students were of the same race and faith. What Lila was actually experiencing was a form of racism. She was being judged and excluded based on her skin color and her different accent and religious practices. She needed to let her parents know how out of place she felt. If the situation became extreme, her best option could have been to enroll in a school that is more diverse.

Whether you are part of the majority or the minority, it is important to learn tolerance and acceptance for diversity. There are many ways that you will be different from other people—in your religious beliefs, skin color, or cultural practices—but even more ways that you are the same.

Imagine if your only choice of ice cream was vanilla. B-o-r-i-n-g! It's the choices that make a trip to your favorite ice-cream shop so fun: pistachio, moose tracks, chocolate chip cookie dough, and caramel crunch. The same goes for people. Invite your Hindu friend over for Christmas, and perhaps she will have you over for a traditional Indian meal. This can bring you closer, showing you how to respect and enjoy your differences while appreciating what you

Get Healthy

1. If you ever find yourself in a very uncomfortable situation, tell someone. If you feel like you're being rejected for who you are, let your parents know what is happening.

2. It's easy to misinterpret people's curiosity as suspicion. If kids are looking at you, it may be just because they want to know more about you. Instead of looking away, smile and see what happens.

3. Try to find a way to share your differences. For example, maybe you could talk to your teacher about doing a presentation on what it is like to be a Hindu—or whatever your difference is. Often kids are more accepting once they have a general understanding.

4. Try to learn about other people's differences. If you show respect for their beliefs, hopefully they will show you the same.

The Last Word from Tamra

Being different from those around you can make you feel isolated. When you feel left out, it's important to find ways to connect with other people. You may find out that you have more in common than you thought. Once people get the chance to know you, the differences between you begin to fade away until they make no difference at all.

8

Fearing Failure

Trying new things is so important because it is the only way you can discover all the many choices you have in life. Some you will try and love, while others you will toss aside as soon as you can. Some you will nail almost the first time you try, and others you will work at and work at and still not quite get. That's the way it's supposed to be!

Of course, even though failure is a necessary part of life, it does not mean we have to like it when it happens. Most of us don't. You can't let it get you down and affect your self-confidence, though. Some things you can just let go. Others you might need to work harder at before you succeed. Either way, you can learn great lessons about your abilities and how wonderfully capable you are!

Samantha found out what failure was like. She did not like it one bit, and she felt lost when it happened to her. What will her goals be now?

Samantha's Story

Samantha looked like she was born to be a gymnast. She was small and slender for her age. She was flexible. Although she wanted to take gymnastics classes when she was little, she lived in a very small city, and she could not find anyone to teach her. Her PE teacher at elementary school didn't know much about the sport other than simple cartwheels or flips, so she couldn't help much. Samantha wanted to know a lot more than that.

Even though failure is a necessary part of life, it does not mean we have to like it when it happens. Most of us don't.

When she got to junior high, she finally had the chance. The school's PE curriculum included a whole unit on gymnastics, and the school even had a gymnastics team that competed against other schools in the area. Samantha couldn't wait to try out. She felt like she already fit right in with the other girls. They reminded her of herself!

On the first day of the gymnastics unit, Mrs. Olsen-Meyer announced that they would be spending the first few weeks on cartwheels, from basic to more advanced types. Samantha could do a basic cartwheel already and was excited to find out they would be learning some more difficult ones. But as the weeks progressed and some girls were doing one-armed and even aerial cartwheels, Samantha was still stuck on basic. She envied the other girls, but the truth was that she was afraid that she would fall and break an arm. Every time she tried, she hesitated at the last moment and couldn't go through with it.

Talk About It

- What mistake is Samantha making? Is she setting herself up to be disappointed? How did that happen?

- Have you ever been positive you would be good at something before you even tried it? How did it turn out?

- Has anyone ever told you that you were born to do something? What was it? Were they right or wrong about it?

Then they moved on to the balance beam. Samantha was looking forward to this. She had been watching gymnasts on television do tricks on balance beams for years, and she couldn't wait to give it a try herself. She could imagine just how graceful she would look.

The first time Samantha tried to hop onto the balance beam, she fell down. The second time she tried to do it, she fell down again. The third time, she was determined to make it, and she did, although she was nowhere close to being graceful.

When she stood up on the balance beam, Samantha found out something about herself that she had never realized. She was afraid of heights! She was scared to look down and sure she was going to fall. This was going to be a problem.

For the next few days, Samantha tried to get over her fear, but it didn't work. It got to the point where she would start to breathe quickly and her heart would beat fast as soon as she saw the balance beam. By the end of the week, Samantha was ready to give up completely. She felt like a total failure. Clearly, gymnastics was not the sport for her. With tears running down her face, she asked Mrs. Olsen-Meyer if she could go home.

Samantha was ready to give up completely. She felt like a total failure.

Talk About It

- **Is Samantha right to give up at this point? What else could she do?**

- **What are some of your fears? What do you do to handle them?**

- **Have you ever felt like a failure at something? What happened next?**

Samantha had an idea about what she wanted to do. Unfortunately, once she had the chance to go for it, she realized that she was not as good as she had imagined. Plus, she had a huge obstacle to overcome—a fear of heights! She was very brave to work on it. Her mistake was thinking that she was a failure for not conquering her fear and becoming a great gymnast.

You will have many, many ambitions in your lifetime. Some you will make happen, and others won't come true. What matters is that you keep dreaming—and dream really, really big dreams! Always do the best you can to reach for the stars. Like Samantha, sometimes you'll realize that an activity is really not for you, or that you are just not skilled enough to accomplish the goal. You then can choose to work and get better at it, or you can let that dream go and reach for another star. Either way, you should keep in mind that failing to accomplish something doesn't make you a failure. It makes you human. It just means that you were meant to pursue a different goal.

Get Healthy

1. If you really want to be good at something and find that you aren't, giving up shouldn't be your first (or second) choice. Instead, you have some other choices. You could get

a tutor or a mentor to help you. You could take extra classes. You could meet with your teacher before or after class. You could study more. And if the skill is new, then practice, practice, practice!

2. If you try to do something and it doesn't work, can you find a similar activity? For example, if being a gymnast doesn't work out, you could try out for cheerleading. If knitting doesn't turn out to be your thing, how about cross-stitch or crochet? There are always other options to explore.

3. Remember that just because you fail at something, it does not mean, in any way, that you are a failure. You will struggle with some skills, but others will come easily to you. Let it go and move on.

The Last Word from Tamra

There's no way around it—failing sucks. But it doesn't have to be a completely rotten experience if you focus on using what you learned to try something else, to improve on what you are doing, or to approach it from a different angle. Failing is simply part of being human—after all, we can't be good at everything. Remember that failing at one thing—or several—does not make you a failure. It makes you human and gives you ideas for what you can try in the future.

9

cutting the Pain

They're called cutters, self-injurers, or "emos." These are the kids who hurt themselves on purpose, cutting themselves with scissors, razors, or fingernails. Some do it for status—and others to stop their emotional pain.

There are two kinds of cutters. Some kids do it to be cool. These kids make light cuts down their arms, legs, or across their wrists. Then they show their friends. If you're in their group, you may have done it or are thinking about doing it to fit in.

These cutters don't want to die or even really hurt themselves. Their reasons for cutting don't have anything to do with a serious psychological condition such as depression. Their problem is that they have very low self-esteem and will do anything to fit in, including harming their own body. These cutters do need help— and should see a psychologist to help them learn to care more about themselves and less about what other kids are doing.

Then there are the cutters who do it in secret. They hide the cutting from everyone who loves them. They do it in hopes that causing physical pain will lessen their emotional pain. They do it expertly, too, disguising the cuts so that no one, not friends, parents, or teachers, sees them. They know where to cut, when to cut, and how to dress to keep it all covered up.

Some kids say they cut because the only way they feel alive is to feel physical pain.

Some kids say they cut because the only way they feel alive is to feel physical pain. Some say that cutting is the best way to take away tension and relieve the pressure of day-to-day living. Sadly, others cut because they are victims of abuse, or because they are suffering from serious psychological problems.

If you're still wondering why they do it, you could ask Rosalyn. She has been cutting herself in secret for almost a year now. So far, she has been able to get away with it, but as summer break gets closer, she is getting

worried. How will she cover up her scars when wearing a tank top and shorts?

Rosalyn's Story

Rosalyn was miserable. It was the kind of beautiful almost-summer day when everyone's mind turned to picnics on the beach, long hikes, and Frisbee games in the park. Rosalyn's friends had asked her to join them at the bike path near her house. She wanted to go but couldn't figure out what to wear. Her usual long-sleeved shirt would look out of place on a day like this. Maybe she could wear a tank top, throw a light jacket over it, and keep it open.

Rosalyn had numerous scars and scabs covering both her arms. They could be found on her legs and belly, too. It was her secret shame that whenever she felt too stressed to cope anymore, she would slide out the razor blade she had stashed inside her diary and, with the bathroom door locked behind her, pick a new place to cut to help relieve the pressure inside.

Talk About It

- **Why does Rosalyn hide what she is doing? What does she mean by "secret shame"?**

- **Do you have a "secret shame"? What is it, and why do you do it?**

- **Have you ever cut yourself? How did it make you feel?**

- **If you're a cutter, does anyone else know? Do you know anyone who cuts herself?**

"Aren't you steamin' in that jacket?" asked Caroline. Rosalyn pretended not to hear the question. Her idea wasn't working.

"Hey, Roz, head's up!" shouted Andrew as he threw the Frisbee her direction. Rosalyn jumped up as high as she could and snatched the plastic disc right out of the air. "You nailed it," Andrew called out, running over to high-five her. As he did, however, he spotted some blood on the arm of her jacket. "Roz, you okay?" he asked. "You're bleeding."

Rosalyn felt her cheeks turn hot with embarrassment and quickly yanked down her sleeve. "I'm fine, Drew," she assured him. "But I gotta get home. It's almost time for lunch." Without giving him a chance to reply, Rosalyn jogged off toward her bike. "I knew that one hadn't healed enough yet," she thought. "Idiot!"

Talk About It

- How did Rosalyn's habit interfere with her having fun with her friends?

- Have you ever lied so that you could get out of an embarrassing situation?

- Has anyone ever noticed your cuts, or have you ever noticed a friend's cuts? How did you handle it?

When Rosalyn got home, she dropped her bike in the driveway and hurried up to her room. No one else was home, which was a relief. Slipping into the bathroom, she locked the door out of habit.

With razor blade in hand, she made the first slice on the inside of her left forearm. The burst of pain was a familiar torture.

With razor blade in hand, she made the first slice on the inside of her

left forearm. The burst of pain was a familiar torture. As it burned, Rosalyn could feel the tension of the moment at the park starting to fade. As she watched the drops of blood slide down her wrist, she felt satisfied and in control. But the next moment, a feeling of shame washed over her. She started to cry, not from the pain, but from the humiliation she felt for having to cut herself and hide her secret from her friends.

Disgusted with herself, Rosalyn quickly bandaged the wound and pulled her sleeve back down to cover it. After splashing some cold water on her face, she went back to her bedroom. There, she noticed a light blinking on her cell phone, which she had thrown on the bed. She had a message.

It was Caroline, and she sounded concerned. "Roz, you there? Everything okay? We were all worried when you left the park in such a hurry, so I just wanted to check on you. If something's wrong, you know you can tell me. Well, I guess I'll talk to ya later."

Rosalyn sat down on her bed and just stared at her phone. As she thought about what to tell her friend, it started to ring. The caller ID showed it was Caroline again. Still unsure what she was going to say, Rosalyn picked up.

Talk About It

- How has Rosalyn made things worse for herself?

- Have you ever been tempted to hurt yourself like Rosalyn? What have you done when you felt that way?

- What advice would you give someone like Rosalyn?

Ask Dr. Vicki

Hurting yourself in any way is never a good way to cope with stress. Girls who self-mutilate, or cut, to relieve their pain and stress are at serious psychological and physical risk. They are in great emotional pain to start. When they cut to relieve the pressure, they only create the additional emotional pain of guilt and shame. This creates a vicious cycle: cutting leads to more emotional pain, which leads to more cutting. As emotional tension builds, the cycle quickens, which leads to more frequent and more serious acts of cutting. The cycle actually creates an addiction to pain, and the need to cut becomes as strong as a junkie's need for the next drug fix.

These girls need help. If you are a cutter or know someone who is cutting, please tell someone. Therapists who specialize in working with cutters can help them break the cycle, decrease the need to cut, and find other ways to deal with stress and tension. Get help!

Get Healthy

1. Find someone you trust and tell them what is going on. Most people who cut themselves need some kind of psychological treatment. Telling a trusted adult will lead you to the help you need.

2. Find another way to respond to stress. Teens who have been treated for cutting suggest taking up some kind of art to keep your hands busy, going for a walk, watching a favorite show or movie, playing with your pet, listening to music, having a good long cry, and starting a journal. Staying around other people also is a great way to prevent yourself from cutting. Every time you feel the urge to hurt yourself, immediately get up and find something else to do to occupy your mind.

3. Try to find a way to lessen the stress you are under. Take a look at all your commitments. Find one or two that you could drop from your schedule. You may have more responsibilities than you are capable of juggling right now, so let go of a couple.

The Last Word from Tamra

People who deliberately hurt themselves are silently crying out for help. Clearly something is driving this pain addiction, which is a killer of self-esteem and personal strength. If you are brave enough to handle the pain of this harmful habit, then use your bravery to reach out and ask for support. The people who love you want to see behind your disguise and help you become the person you really want to be.

10
Ending It All

As amazing—and tragic—as it may seem, suicide is the third leading cause of teenage death in this country. For every successful attempt—meaning the person kills him or herself—twenty-five others fail—meaning they live. Those are scary numbers. What could possibly make life so difficult that dying is seen as the only solution?

When it comes to suicide, a big difference exists between girls and boys. Boys succeed at it more often, while girls attempt it more often. Girls are more likely to change their minds after taking pills or cutting their wrists and call for help before it is too late. Boys usually use methods such as shooting or hanging themselves that work very quickly, leaving them without that option.

The desperately sad thing is that there is no problem that cannot be overcome one way or another if you are determined enough. There are solutions, alternatives, choices, ideas, and resources everywhere you turn. Usually all you have to do is reach out and ask for help, and the people who love and care about you will do anything in their power to provide it.

Let's face it, all kids feel down sometimes. Adults experience this, too. It's a natural part of life, just like failure. But normal sadness comes and then goes, sometimes teaching valuable lessons in the process. Depression that stays, however, is **Depression that stays is not supposed to be a part of life. It's a warning sign that something is terribly wrong.** not supposed to be a part of life. It's a warning sign that something is terribly wrong. Please, pay attention to it.

Desiree didn't. She had overlooked the signs for months that she was suffering from depression. She didn't just have a lousy day—she couldn't remember not having a lousy day. She was in a downward spiral that ended in a very dangerous place.

Desiree's Story

Desiree paged through her journal. Over the past few months, she had written less and drawn more. She

knew her mother would go nuts if she saw some of her sketches. Even she could see they had a theme—death. It was what she thought about most of the time, and her obsession was reflected in her sketches of guns, nooses, coffins, headstones, and bottles of pills.

Just the other day, she had given her best friend Julia her favorite tote and a pair of silver earrings, telling Jules she wanted her to have the gifts because they were "BFF." That night she'd even written out her own form of a will. She left her clothes and the rest of her jewelry to Julia, who wore the same size as she did in everything but shoes, and her books to her geeky little brother, who always wanted to borrow them.

Rolling halfway off her bed, Desiree took a bite of the sandwich her mom had made for her lunch. Her parents were always complaining that she did not eat meals at the table with them anymore, but sitting with them was too much trouble. They asked her too many questions and seemed to want to look deep inside her where she didn't allow anyone to go. If they found out about her grades this fall, they would stop asking questions and just ground her.

Talk About It

- **What signs show how dangerous Desiree's depression has become?**

- **Have you ever not wanted people to be able to see into your head because they wouldn't like what they saw?**

- **Have you ever been really depressed? What did you do?**

- **Do you know anyone like Desiree? How could you help that person?**

Desiree checked her e-mail, but there was nothing new. She surfed over to her MySpace page but didn't feel like adding anything to last month's entry. Nothing worthwhile ever happened to her, so why post? Her friends didn't even seem to notice if she added anything or not.

Restless, Desiree looked out the window of her room. Great, more rain. Just what she needed.

Flipping through the numbers in her cell phone directory, Desiree thought about calling Julia but then decided not to. What would she say? "Hey, Julia, wanna hang out with me because I am incredibly depressed?" What kind of invitation was that?

Talk About It

- Why is Desiree restless? What is her attitude toward everything?

- Why do you think she wants to call Julia? What stops her from doing it?

- If you could talk to Desiree, what would you tell her?

Desiree grabbed her can of soda and walked into the bathroom. She opened the medicine cabinet, looking for her hairbrush. Instead, her eyes fell upon the row of medications lined up inside. There were the leftover pills from when she had mono, the pills her mom took every day for her migraine headaches, and the pain pills left over from her dad's surgery last year.

Slowly, she looked through all the bottles. She realized that all together, she had a lot of powerful drugs right in front of her. As if in a dream, Desiree began twisting the top off each one and spilling the tablets

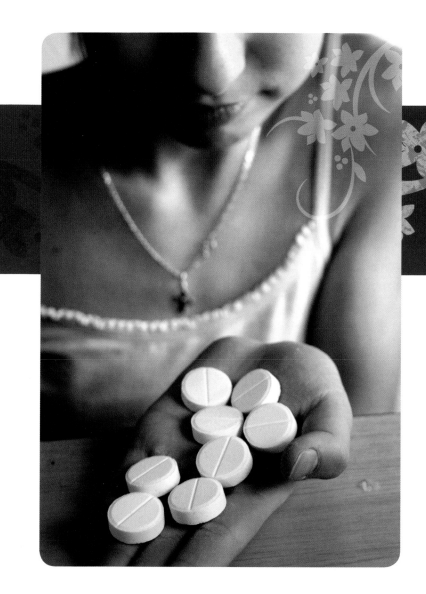

into her hand. She was fascinated by the rainbow of colors in her palm.

With a jerk, Desiree threw all the pills into her mouth. She began gulping her soda as fast as she could to wash them all down. When they were gone, she grabbed pills from another three bottles and took those.

Finally, she went back into her room and lay down on her bed. She felt very quiet inside—almost at peace. A little later, she realized she was starting to fall asleep. She knew what that meant. The pills were doing their job. Now, the time had come to make that important decision: go to sleep and not wake up again, or run into the bathroom and make herself throw up. Throwing up meant explaining herself and letting others know what she had done. It meant facing the pain that was hiding deep inside. It meant waking up tomorrow morning with the same ache. Sleeping sure sounded a lot easier.

The time had come to make that important decision: go to sleep and not wake up again, or run into the bathroom and make herself throw up.

Talk About It

- Why did Desiree decide to take the pills? What do you think is going to happen next?

- What other choices did Desiree have in this situation?

- Have you ever considered committing suicide? Why? Have you told anyone about how you feel? If not, why not?

- Have you ever had a friend who talked about suicide? What did you do?

Severe depression leaves you feeling helpless to do anything about it, and hopeless that things will ever be any different. Kids who think about suicide are looking for an easy way to escape from emotional pain or a situation that seems as though it will never get better. Desiree had shown signs of sinking deeper and deeper into depression that nobody picked up on. Spending more and more time alone, withdrawing from friends and family, giving away possessions, and letting grades drop are all signs that a kid is in real trouble.

While many girls at one time or another say things like, "I wish I was dead," most don't want to die. They are just really upset. But the girls who think, write, and draw about it, and even start planning ways to carry it out are at great risk of making a suicide attempt.

Nothing is worth dying over. That's the depression talking. No matter what is happening in your life, no matter how terrible it might seem, you can get through it with the help of the people who love you, along with trained professionals. With therapy and possibly medication, you will feel less depressed and see your situation more clearly. You will realize that killing yourself is not the solution to anything—it's just the start of pain and suffering for the people you leave behind.

Get Healthy

1. The number one way to stop suicide from happening is by telling someone how you are feeling. It is extremely important that you speak up the first time a suicidal thought goes through your mind. Tell a friend, parent, teacher, counselor, neighbor, relative—someone.

2. Realize that suicide is permanent. You can't take it back once you feel better or happier.

3. If you ever have a friend who tells you she wants to kill herself, and then makes you promise not to tell anyone, do it anyway. This is one promise you should never keep. It's better to have a friend who is alive and pissed off at you than one who is dead.

The Last Word from Tamra

Life is challenging, puzzling, unfair, cruel, and tragic—but it is also beautiful, loving, silly, gentle, and wonderful. The only way you can know that is to face your sadness, fight it, and let yourself become a stronger person than ever before. It means having the self-confidence, the self-esteem, and the personal strength to look life right in the eye and tell it, "I'm here to stay, and boy, are you lucky to have me!"

A Second Look

As you process the stories in this book and how they relate to your own life, take a moment to consider what it means to have personal strength. No two girls would answer the same way, but they'd probably agree it has a lot to do with being true to yourself. As you mature and face more and more complicated situations and start to make your own decisions, try to listen hard to that ever-developing internal compass. You need to be comfortable standing up for what you believe in and what you know is right, taking responsibility for your actions, and working toward the goals you set for yourself.

Does that sound like a tall order when it seems like all you can manage is keeping up with your schoolwork, blending in with the crowd, and keeping your parents off your back? Don't be too hard on yourself. Personal strength also has a lot do with giving yourself some slack, accepting your strengths and weaknesses, and learning to face your failures with grace.

You might think girls like Rosalyn and Desiree have no personal strength. But it takes enormous courage to stop a cycle of self-destruction and get help. If these girls are able to conquer their harmful impulses, they'll probably end up even stronger for having gone through their ordeals.

So do you have personal strength? Don't feel like you have to answer immediately. We're all beautiful works in progress. As long as you strive to be true to yourself in everything you do, chances are the answer soon will be yes.

XOXO,
Tamra

Pay It Forward

Remember, a healthful life is about balance. Now that you know how to walk that path, pay it forward to a friend or even to yourself! Remember the Get Healthy tips throughout this book, and then take these steps to get healthy and get going.

- The next time you're feeling down on yourself, don't keep the feelings to yourself. Talk it over with a close friend or family member who you trust.

- Everyone has a special talent. If you're not sure what yours might be, think about what activities you most enjoy. What makes you happiest? Chances are you'll find your strengths there.

- Pay attention to your instincts. Don't let yourself be pressured into doing something you don't want to do just to fit in.

- Always be true to yourself, and don't be afraid to stand up for what you believe in. But remember to be respectful of people whose ideas differ from yours. Having opinions is fine, but forcing them on others isn't cool.

- It is normal to start thinking about your sexuality at this age. Remember that whether you are gay or straight is just one part of who you are. It doesn't define you as a person.

- If you don't succeed at first at something you really want to do, don't give up right away. Think of ways you could overcome the challenge: getting a tutor, studying more, or taking extra classes, for example.

- If you're uncomfortable talking to someone new, try to maintain eye contact even if you're not feeling confident. This makes a stronger connection and helps put people at ease.

- Make a point of learning about other people's differences. If you show respect for their be-liefs, hopefully they will show you the same. And learning about other cultures, religions, foods, and dress can add variety to your life.

- Self-destructive habits such as cutting can be signs of a serious psychological disorder. If you or someone you know cuts, tell someone you trust. In the meantime, look for other ways to relieve your stress—such as play-ing with a pet, listening to music, or starting a journal.

- The number one way to prevent suicide is to tell someone. No matter how bad things may seem, nothing is worth dying over. Therapy and possibly medication can help relieve the pain of depression. If you or a friend is de-pressed or having suicidal thoughts, do not keep it a secret.

Additional Resources

Selected Bibliography

Barker, Molly. *Girls on Track: A Parent's Guide to Inspiring Our Daughters to Achieve a Lifetime of Self-Esteem and Respect*. New York, NY: Ballantine Books, 2004.

Deal, Joann. *Girls Will Be Girls: Raising Confident and Courageous Daughters*. New York, NY: Hyperion, 2003.

Nelson, Gary E. *A Relentless Hope: Surviving the Storm of Teen Depression*. Eugene, OR: Cascade Books, 2007.

Further Reading

Beck, Debra. *My Feet Aren't Ugly!: A Girl's Guide to Loving Herself from the Inside Out*. New York, NY: Beaufort Books, 2007.

Cochran, Lauren Hoffman. *Unbecoming Stephanie*. Burlington, MA: JAC Publishing, 2005.

Gray, Heather M. and Samantha Phillips. *Real Girls Real World: A Guide to Finding Your True Self*. Emeryville, CA: Seal Press, 2005.

Naik, Anita. *Wise Guides: Self-Esteem*. London, England: Hodder and Stoughton, 2005.

Nelson, Richard E. *The Power to Prevent Suicide: A Guide for Teens Helping Teens*. Minneapolis, MN: Free Spirit Publishing, 2006.

Web Sites

To learn more about personal strength and self-acceptance, visit ABDO Publishing Company on the World Wide Web **at www.abdopublishing.com**. Web sites about personal strength and self-acceptance are featured on our Book Links page. These links are routinely monitored and updated to provide the most current information available.

For More Information

For more information on this subject, contact or visit the following organizations.

I Am B.E.A.U.T.I.F.U.L.

I AM, INC.
4850 Golden Parkway, Suite B-230, Buford, GA 30518
404-545-9051
www.iambeautiful.org
The group features an annual Unsung Heroine Award, as well as national programs, volunteer opportunities, and camps.

National Suicide Prevention Lifeline

1-800-273-8255
This 24-hour, toll-free hotline is available to anyone in a suicidal crisis.

SAVE—Suicide Awareness Voices of Education

8120 Penn Ave. S., Suite 470, Bloomington, MN 55431
952-946-7998
www.save.org
A nonprofit organization, SAVE strives to raise awareness of depression and suicide through education.

Glossary

attitude
> A person's opinions or feelings about someone or something.

confident
> Having a strong belief in your own abilities.

consequences
> Results of an action.

depression
> A psychological disorder marked by sadness, inactivity, difficulty concentrating, feelings of hopelessness, and sometimes suicidal tendencies.

expectation
> A thought that something ought to happen.

Hindu
> A person who follows Hinduism, an India-based religion that focuses on multiple gods and goddesses.

homosexuality
> Being sexually attracted and in romantic relationships with people of the same sex.

identity
> The character and personality of an individual.

lesbian
> A homosexual woman.

petition

A letter signed by many people asking those in power to change their policy or actions or telling them how the signers feel about a certain issue or situation.

phobia

An extremely strong fear.

pressure

Strong influence, force, or persuasion; a burden or a strain.

self-esteem

A feeling of personal pride and of respect for oneself.

self-injurers

People who release their stress through some form of hurting or injuring themselves.

Index

About the Author

Tamra Orr is the author of more than 100 educational books for young people, including *When the Mirror Lies (Eating Disorders)* and *Halls of Violence, Halls of Hope (School Violence)*. Orr lives in the Pacific Northwest with her husband and four kids, ranging in age from 12 to 24.

Photo Credits

Jeremy Hohengarten/iStockphoto, 12; Lawrence Sawyer/iStockphoto, 15; Andrew Manley/iStockphoto, 17; Carmen Martínez Banús/iStockphoto, 23; Yellow Dog Productions/Getty Images, 25; Laurenc Gough/iStockphoto, 27; Image Source/AP Images, 32, 37, 42, 69; Brandon Laufenberg/iStockphoto, 47; Bonnie Jacobs/iStockphoto, 52; Bart Coenders/iStockphoto, 55; Lisa F. Young/iStockphoto, 61; Jupiterimages/AP Images, 63; Mel Yates/Getty Images, 71; Rick Egan/AP Images, 77; Dragan Trifunovic/iStockphoto, 79; Kris Russell/iStockphoto, 84; Lauren Greenfield/AP Images, 87; Ana-Maria Diaconescu/iStockphoto, 89; Jason Lugo/iStockphoto, 94; Elena Itsenko/iStockphoto, 97; iStockphoto, 99